Don't Curse Your Relationship or Marriage

Wisdom Realms

Published by Wisdom Realms Publications, 2023.

Table of Contents

DEDICATION

I dedicate this book to all married couples, those aspiring to get married and all who want what God has destined for them in their relationship and/or marriage.

FOREWORD

───

God has raised Wisdom Realms with a unique and profound message and grace to make great multigenerational impact in the body of Christ and the world at large.

After reading **'Don't Curse your Relationship or Marriage'**, I realized God has endowed him with an incredible insight into the challenges of marriages and relationships. He shares deep understanding of the power of words and the impact they have on marriages and relationships.

In this book, you will be informed and equipped to deal with challenges like offences, unforgiveness, abuse and the effects of negative words that has plagued many relationships and thrown many families into chaos.

I guarantee that you will benefit immensely from the God given insight in this book.

Reverend Prince K. Monovis

FaithHouse Chapel Int'l - The Wonders Cathedral

Tse Addo Roundabout – Accra

INTRODUCTION

Being a Christian does not mean you will have the best by default even though you are entitled to it. The words you utter create an atmosphere that determines if the things in your life will thrive or die. Words are very powerful and affect every sphere of life.

What you are about to read in this book was borne from an experience and seeks to draw your attention to the effect of the words that proceed out of your mouth in your relationship or marriage. It was one evening in June 2011.

My girlfriend at the time and I had a misunderstanding one night about something I cannot even remember today. Words were spoken without thinking about their effects. Indeed, tempers were over the roof. After the argument, we called it a night and went to our various homes.

I lay on my bed immediately I got home and started replaying the events in my mind.

Around midnight, the Lord visited me and ceased the moment to educate and enlighten me extensively on the dangerous effects of words on relationships and marriages. I was really surprised.

I quickly grabbed my pen and an exercise book and started to write the deep insights God was giving me. My attention was drawn to the choice of words that were used earlier that night like a magnet draws a piece of metal. In my mind, I thought it was just emotions being voiced out. But I was wrong. Little did I know that curses were flying about.

The lesson from God that night has stayed with me all these years because He gave me deep insight into the dangerous effect of what happened earlier that evening. I must say that I was really surprised. God precipitated the lessons that night on the words that we spoke and subsequently taught me that ***no one waters a plant with hot water who wants it to grow and bear fruits.***

After that night, I was very careful of what I said in a relationship no matter what happened. I understood that ***being careless when it comes to words can rob you of the glory of your destiny.*** It has been more than a decade but I still remember that night as though it was yesterday. The encounter opened my eyes on the power and impact of words.

As a Christian, one thing I have come to understand is that ***whatever you curse cannot survive.*** Words carry great power no matter how they are uttered and by whom. ***You cannot curse a tree and then expect it to bring forth for you.*** What you kill with your words cannot continue to breathe.

You cannot water a plant with hot water and expect it to survive. It is just not possible. As I almost did on the night I received this insight, a lot of people have unfortunately killed promising relationships and marriages through words. And the sad part is that they do not even know what they have done to themselves. But this book carries the message of hope and restoration.

This book exposes one of the often disregarded but powerful weapons the devil has used against believers for ages. You will discover the power and effect words can have on your life. Truly, you can walk in every level of greatness you want for your relationship or marriage. The key, however, is that *you must use your words right*.

I am delighted to share this insight with you. Enjoy the wisdom of God as you swim through the pages.

CHAPTER ONE
THE CONCEPT OF RELATIONSHIP AND MARRIAGE

Relationship or marriage is a beautiful thing. They can bring a certain level of joy and happiness that people otherwise would not have in their lives.

It is, however, worth mentioning that not everybody gets to experience this joy and happiness they bring for several reasons. Some of these reasons are what we are going to delve into in this book.

The concept or idea of relationships and marriages was brought forth by God in the garden of Eden. According to the Bible, after God created Adam, He realized it was bad for him to be alone. To remedy the situation, God brought Eve into the picture.

He created Eve as a companion for Adam so that he would not be alone.

21 And the LORD God caused a deep sleep to fall upon Adam, and he slept: and he took one of his ribs, and closed up the flesh instead thereof;

22 And the rib, which the LORD God had taken from man, made he a woman, and brought her unto the man.

DON'T CURSE YOUR RELATIONSHIP OR MARRIAGE

Genesis 2:21-22

Anytime I read this text, my imaginations run wild. I ask myself, *"What was God's motive or intention for bringing the two together? Was it for their good or doom? Was it meant to be a blessing or a curse?"*

I believe you will agree with me that it was for their good. God bringing Eve to Adam in the garden was meant to be a blessing, not a curse. What this simply means is that in God's mind, when a man and a woman come together in a relationship or marriage, *according to His will,* the result should be a blessing.

But if that is the case, then why do some relationships or marriages experience the opposite? Why at all do some promising ones sometimes fall on the rocks all of a sudden?

Well, there are a lot of reasons ranging from spiritual to physical. For a good thing to end up bad all of a sudden, it means that something has gone wrong.

It means that something has interfered with its state.

One of the reasons many marriages and relationships fail is the lack of understanding of people concerning God's concept on the subject.

One of the lessons I learnt that night is that ***marriage or relationship is God's idea and not man's.*** For that reason, He is very concerned about everything about your relationship or marriage - including *how* you even talk to your partner and the things you say to them. This is because He wants you to walk in His divine idea for establishing them.

This understanding puts you in a place to know that God is concerned about what He births. ***That it is His idea means God has destined it to be a great blessing.*** But some people miss out on the blessing because they get involved with people who are not in His *will* for their lives. That is against God's idea.

In other words, when people get yoked to others He has not brought to them or approved for their lives, they are fighting His idea. The danger of this is that these people are operating outside or against God's idea.

It means they would not have what it takes to help or complement each other to fulfill destiny. ***God is very much concerned about who you are involved with*** because at the end of the day, it sets the tone for the success or failure of relationships or marriages.

He is aware that those who get involved with others outside His idea will be deficient when it comes to each other's destinies. Therefore, such relationships or marriages often suffer a natural death with time.

Of a truth, ***marriage and relationship are beautiful things, but you cannot get involved with anybody just because you want to experience it.*** That is not God's idea. Notice from the text we read that it was God who *brought* Eve to Adam, not Adam went for Eve.

What it means is that she was in God's *will* for him. Now, you may want to ask, *"But some people get involved with and marry others in the will of God for their lives yet such marriages and relationships still fail. Why?"*

DON'T CURSE YOUR RELATIONSHIP OR MARRIAGE

One of the major reasons, though often disregarded, is how we use words without thinking about their consequences or effects. Oftentimes, people do not know the reason God brings others into their lives, and that is where the problem generally begins.

You can destroy a good thing with your words when you don't know why you have it in the first place.

CHAPTER TWO
GOD'S WORK IS PERFECT

In order to appreciate the negative effect words can have on relationships or marriages, it is very important to understand first and foremost that God's creations are and have always been perfect.

We know that God created the world and everything in it. But the question is in what *state* were these things when they were created? Were they good or bad? Were they perfect or imperfect?

God's work is and has always been perfect. There is no blemish in Him. Therefore, there cannot be a mistake in what He does. One truth every Christian must grow to understand is that ***God is always the author of perfection.***

He is a perfect God and everything that comes from Him is perfect. It means that His plan for all His children is clothed in perfection. Let's take a look at these scriptures from the Bible:

And God saw everything that he had made, and behold, it was very good. And there was evening and there was morning, a sixth day.

Genesis 1:31 (RSV)

Be ye therefore perfect, even as your Father which is in heaven is perfect.

DON'T CURSE YOUR RELATIONSHIP OR MARRIAGE

Matthew 5:48

As for God, his way is perfect: the word of the LORD is tried: he is a buckler to all those that trust in him.

Psalms 18:30

The text of scriptures above and several others attest to the undeniable perfection of God. They paint a picture of His perfection in everything He does. **God is perfect and can never be the author of imperfection.** He perfects imperfections in our lives.

Imperfection cannot be found in God. He is flawless and demands that we are perfect as well **(Matthew 5:48)**. *Perfection cannot produce imperfection.* In fact, a perfect God cannot bring forth imperfection. Nothing He does is imperfect or wrong.

Everything He did, is doing, and is about to do is absolutely perfect. There is absolutely no blemish in Him. Therefore, there can never be a mistake in what He does.

By implication, it means that the relationships and/or marriages of Christians are destined according to the *will* of God and are inherently perfect. Now, I know this may sound awkward and unbelievable to some of you, but it is the truth.

Every provision of God for His children in His plan is perfect. This is one truth I have grown to believe and so must you. *Everything God does concerning my life is perfect* even if I fail to see it that way. They fall within the lines of His perfection. Let us take a look at what the Bible says:

Every good gift and every perfect gift is from above, and cometh down from the Father of lights, with whom is no variableness, neither shadow of turning.

James 1:17

First of all, the scripture we just read says *every* gift, not *some*. Then it says it is *perfect*, not imperfect. Relationships and marriages are part of God's gifts to His children. It simply means they are perfect by nature. **They are not free from challenges, but they are without defect.**

A gift is something you receive and I cannot imagine God giving an imperfect relationship or marriage to any of His children. The reason is that **every plan He has for His children is perfect**. His thought for you is firmly rooted in His perfection (**Jeremiah 29:11**).

I understand that **I may have an imperfect partner, but it does not mean what God has destined for me is imperfect.** Everything God does and plans to do in your life is perfect because that is who He is. Even so, it is important to know that **you could mar these perfect things through your words, actions and inactions**. You could destroy every good thing God has set out to do with the words of your mouth.

That, beloved, is the reason you must **learn to speak well to experience perfection in your relationship or marriage**. Your words will either keep you in the planes of perfection or bury you in the ashes of imperfection.

DON'T CURSE YOUR RELATIONSHIP OR MARRIAGE

Wrong words will destroy perfection and put any marriage or relationship in recession no matter its prospects.

You may want to ask, *"If everything about God's plan for my life is perfect, how come there seems to be a lot of imperfections surrounding me?"*

Well, that is a good question and the Bible provides us with the right answer. Let us take a look at how the Bible answers this question in the next chapter.

CHAPTER THREE
UNDERSTANDING A CURSE

———

On the night of the encounter with the Lord, I learnt that *a curse is anything that negates positivity*. In other words, it is anything that is inherently evil or prevents progress.

It is a seal of limitation, a bondage or a blockade set in place by the words or actions or inactions of man to block, decrease or place a limit on the progress or development of a thing. In other words, it means doing things to disrupt the progress of a thing.

The Oxford Advanced Learners Dictionary (Sixth Edition) defines a curse as:

• A rude or offensive word or phrase that some people use when they are angry.

• A word or phrase that has a magic power to make something bad happen.

• Something (word or actions) that causes harm or evil.

From the above definitions from the dictionary, we can simply define a curse as *a spoken word or action taken to make something good to be bad.* It is any word that has the potential or capacity to spoil a good thing. Thus, it can change a thing from good to bad.

DON'T CURSE YOUR RELATIONSHIP OR MARRIAGE

We can also see that such offensive words or phrases are used by some people, not everybody. In other words, such words are used by people who fail to control their tongues when they are angry.

It is important to note that curses do not only come through words *(what is said)*; they can also come through actions *(what we do)* and inactions *(what we fail or refuse to do)*.

It is sad but true to say that many people, including Christians, have cursed and reduced relationships or marriages they are involved in to the ground by the unskillful and immature use of words. They have marred (destroyed) the glory and honour of their unions with the bullets of evil and unsavoury words through callousness.

You must understand that ***the tongue has the power to cause great havoc to a man's destiny.*** As little as it is, the tongue can change the whole course of a man's life in a millisecond through words.

That is the reason I often tell people, ***"The fact that God has destined or prepared good things for you does not mean they will come to pass as destined by Him."*** It takes a lot to manifest God's plan for a person.

But unfortunately, we live in a generation where some people believe and teach others that nothing can stop or prevent the blessings and plan of God for an indivivual. Well, that is not entirely true. ***You are powerful enough to sabotage God's agenda for your life***, and that is what a lot of people do not know.

You can place a stumbling block to and talk yourself out of the blessings God has in store for you. I think the message these people want to communicate is that *the plan of God to bless us is unchanging,* and that is true. But the other truth is that *whether it will come to pass or not greatly depends on you.*

In other words, *God's plan to bless you will not change, but the manifestation is liable to change.* It means if God plans to give you a house, it is forever established before Him to do it. But whether that plan will manifest or not depends on you. Do you understand that?

Men do not understand what a powerful thing it is to be created in God's image and likeness (**Genesis 1:26-27**). Being created in His image and likeness means that *you possess the power to be or place a stumbling block to the things God wants to do in your life* in so many ways, key among them being through the unskillful use of words.

But that is not God's intention for creating us in His image and likeness. For instance, the Bible clearly states that Jesus could not perform any miracles in his hometown, except to heal a few people because of their unbelief (**Matthew 6:5**). The Bible was specific about what led to that - their *unbelief.*

It means *the actions of man can mar God's plan.* It was the people that limited or prevented Jesus Christ from performing miracles among them. He wanted to, but He could not because they did not allow Him. How did they prevent Him? Through unbelief. And take note that miracles are part of the blessing package of God for His children.

DON'T CURSE YOUR RELATIONSHIP OR MARRIAGE

That is how powerful man is. So, if nothing can stop God from blessing man like some people believe and teach, why then were they able to prevent Jesus Christ from performing miracles? Is Jesus Christ not the Son of God and God by all standards?

Did He not come to earth to do what God would have done for humanity if He were here in person? So, what happened? Curses! Curses are the products of words, actions, and inactions. The devil often uses words as a major weapon to deny people their blessing. *He uses the words of men to set them up for destruction.*

With it, he has ensnared many and ensured that they do not see the beauty of what God has destined for them. Through words, Satan fights the relationships and marriages of people. Get this - *the devil uses the unsavoury words of others and the negative words you speak to limit you.*

He has empowered people to impede the destinies of others through words. And while it may be easier to deal with the curse others place on you through their words, it can sometimes be difficult to deal with the ones you established by your own words and actions.

Understand this – *the curse you place on yourself is more powerful and dangerous than those anybody can place on you.* That is why it is easier to avert or undo the evil words of others against you than those you utter against yourself.

Most times, people are not even aware that they are cursing themselves with their words.

A lot of people who complain about the misfortunes surrounding their relationships or marriages are not aware that they are the architects of their problems. They do not know that they planted the seeds through their words. They have defiled the power of words and underestimated the power of God residing in them.

No matter who you are, **when you defile the power of words,** underestimate the power of God residing in you and speak anyhow, **you place curses on your path in life**.

According to the Bible, **every word declared by the tongue is bound to come to pass with time** – whether negative or positive (**Job 22:28**). There is no word the tongue speaks that will not be established. That is the reason I am of the opinion that the power behind the tongue is one of the first truths or lessons people ought to be exposed to before marriage or a relationship.

The reason is that at the end of the day, your words will either make or destroy what you have. Unlike what most people usually perceive to be the case, **you do not have to perform a ritual to be bound by a curse.** Your words are enough to enshroud your marital or relationship destiny with the darkness or gloom of curses.

Always remember what a curse is and guard your mouth. If your words will not bring progress to your love life, do not utter them. If your words have the potential to destroy your relationship or marriage, do not utter them. In fact, just shut up!

CHAPTER FOUR
EXERCISING THE POWER OF THOUGHTS AND WORDS

P ower is good, but dangerous. The reason is that it can be exercised wrongly. And when that happens, it brings pain, discomfort, and affliction.

To exercise power simply means to put it to use. It means to engage it in order to achieve a particular result. From scripture, we see how man exercised his power.

*And our of the ground the LORD GOD formed every beast of the field and every bird of the sky, **and brought them to the man to see what he would call them; and whatever the man called a living creature, that was its name.***

Genesis 2:19 (NASB)

The scripture above contains a very profound lesson we must learn if we intend to keep our relationships and marriages in the perfect state God made them. In fact, we cannot do away with it if we expect to walk in relationship and marital perfection.

Before we continue, let me clarify something very important – every relationship or marriage has its peculiar challenges. But that does not render them imperfect. In other words, ***our relationships and/or marriages do not go through challenges because they are imperfect.***

To think in that line is to prepare your mind for an unhappy journey of love which is something nobody wants. The message is simple – relationships and marriages are perfect in their nature or originality no matter the challenges one encounter.

Perfection does not in any way mean the absence of challenges. A relationship or marriage is perfect no matter the challenges partners encounter. Despite the challenges, you still have a perfect relationship or marriage *(if you are in God's will)*. If you are not in God's *will*, then you are not in His perfect plan.

Now, after God created the beasts and birds, *He brought them to Adam to see what he would call them*. Remember, we learnt earlier that everything God does is perfect. So, it means that He brought perfect creations to Adam to name.

This paints a vivid picture of God giving His perfect finished work to us – His children. What does it mean to name a thing and what goes into it?

To name a thing is *to assign a word(s) to it, or to give it an identity*. It also means *to express your opinion about it*. Identity gives characteristics to things. In other words, your opinion becomes the reputation of that thing.

We read earlier that everything God made was good (**Genesis 1:31**). This scripture is further buttressed in **Psalms 18:30**. Now, God created the beasts and birds and He brought them to Adam to see what he would call them. It is important we understand or take notice of this.

DON'T CURSE YOUR RELATIONSHIP OR MARRIAGE

By implication, it means Adam was given perfect creations to name. And notice what the Bible says... *and whatever the man called a living creature, that was its name.* The Bible does not say that God told Adam what to call the living creatures. He called them what he wanted them to be identified by.

Here, we can see that Adam was given the authority to name or give identity to God's perfect creation. What do you think would have happened if he had given bad names to these creations? I hope you are seeing the picture clearly?

Even though everything was good, it would have been bad if he had named them otherwise. This establishes the agelong truth that ***God gives His perfect finished work to His children, but what it becomes at the end of the day depends on them***. He delivers into your hands everything just as He made them – in their perfection.

Now, ***your duty as a recipient of what God created is to maintain its perfection.*** You are to fight and make sure that the perfection of what you have been given is not lost through your words or actions. Do you understand that assignment? The Bible says that whatsoever Adam called a living creature, that was its name. What are you calling your relationship or marriage?

From this, it is obvious God took the words of Adam just as he spoke them. This represents the influence of man on divine perfection. ***Every human being on earth has a level of power they exercise in their daily activities through what they say or do***. And it is in the exercising of this power that many people unknowingly create problems for themselves.

From the story of Adam, our attitudes, actions and/or inactions can render imperfect the prefect intents of God for our lives. Do you remember how the people prevented Jesus from performing miracles in their midst? Let me ask you this question...what labels are you knowingly or unknowingly putting on your relationship or marriage? Do you speak ill or well of it?

To keep our relationships or marriages in the perfect state God gave them to us, *we need to exercise the power of thoughts and words rightly*. When God brought the creation to Adam to see what he would call them, He was asking him to express his opinion. He was asking for his view and the Bible tells us that *...and whatever the man called a living creature, that was its name.*

The lesson here is strictly on *thoughts* and *words*. But we cannot really talk about words without first touching on thoughts. Your thoughts also play an important role when it comes to your relationship and/or marriage. It sets the tone for what may or may not happen in your union.

Thoughts give birth to words and determine the way you behave in your relationship or marriage. Your thoughts about a thing become your words in favour or against it.

Having negative thoughts about your relationship or marriage, yourself or your partner is programing everything for failure or doom (**Proverbs 23:7**). The reason? *Your thoughts become confessions and also dictate your actions.* So, if Adam's words, borne out of the image and likeness of God inside him and his thoughts were established by God, then you do not need to be told that your thoughts and every word you utter will be established as well.

The truth is that *the image and likeness of God cannot utter evil words*. Therefore, anytime you say anything evil about your relationship or marriage, it means you are speaking outside the image and likeness of God inside you. It means that you are not speaking out of revelation from God.

Adam's experience with God tells us how powerful our thoughts and words are. He spoke like God out of the ability and capacity of God within him. *When Adam spoke, it was like God speaking and his words could not be denied*. Whatever he said took effect because he was created in the image and likeness - the two powerful sides - of God (**Genesis 1:26-27**).

And so are you. It tells you that your thoughts and words are held in high esteem and established in the realms of the spirit, whatever they may be. Look at what the Bible says:

Thou shalt also decree a thing, and it shall be established unto thee: and the light shall shine upon thy ways.

Job 22:28

This scripture is basically telling you that anything you say will come to pass. At the latter part, it speaks about light shining on your ways, but the opposite is also very true. *Light cannot shine on your way when the words you utter are not healthy.*

Though everything was perfect, it would have been otherwise if Adam had named them so. *God gave a perfect creation, but Adam could have made it imperfect.* We have to fight and make sure that the perfection of what we have been given is not lost through our words and actions.

Never forget this statement – *whatsoever Adam called a living creature, that was its name.* You possess the same power Adam had when he was in the Garden of Eden. **Whatsoever you call a thing becomes its name.** Whatever you call your relationship or marriage, that will be its name.

It is one principle God has always respected from the beginning of time. He took the words of Adam seriously and did not change what he called the creation He brought to him.

He endorsed every word to the letter. It shows the level of influence you have on divine perfection. It proves that attitudes, actions, and/or inactions can render the perfect gift or intents of God imperfect.

Again, I ask, *"What label are you putting on your relationship or marriage?"* What are your words doing to your relationship or marital destiny? Let us take a look at what God says in the book of Jeremiah:

> *For I know the thoughts that I think towards you, saith the Lord, thoughts of peace and not of evil, to give you an expected end.*

Jeremiah 29:11

The thoughts of God are without flaw or defect. They contain His expectations or best for your life as determined beforehand by Him. So you are not called to live a life that is not planned. **Every detail of your life has been carefully planned by God for your good.**

DON'T CURSE YOUR RELATIONSHIP OR MARRIAGE

Do you know that God cares about what you think or say? He is because He framed the world we see out of words. He knows the power behind them. He used them as raw materials to create the things we see.

By faith, ***we see the world called into existence by God's word,***
what we see is created by what we don't see.

Hebrews 11:3 (MSG)

God called the world into existence through words (**Genesis 1:3, 5, 9,**). *We cannot see words but we can feel their effects.* We cannot see words with our eyes, but they create things. ***Anytime we think or speak, we create things.*** Whether they come out good or bad depends on the content of our thoughts or words. Use your words to create the kind of relationship or marriage you want.

Evil thoughts and careless words will create bad experiences in your relationship or marriage. ***Bad experiences in life do not fall from the sky;*** they are created through thoughts and words. ***A positive thought or word can change all negative occurrences in your life.*** It can reprogramme your entire life to produce good fruits.

The opposite is also very true. The Bible says as a man thinks, so is he (**Proverbs 23:7**). Everything is the product of thoughts or words. ***The way you think is ultimately the way you will speak.*** And what you say can change the course of your destiny from good to bad. Beware!

CHAPTER FIVE
THE EFFECT OF WORDS

The *effect* of a word is the result it produces after it has been spoken. It is the power it has to cause a thing to happen. Words generally have two effects – *positive* and *negative*.

A positive word will give a positive effect and vice versa. **One of the things about the effect of words is that it works whether you are born again or not.** It is like planting a seed. You do not have to be a farmer before a seed you plant germinates.

A farmer or not, a seed you put in the earth will grow and bear. In a similar vein, **whatever a person says will come to pass whether they are born again or not.** One thing I have realized is that there is no place for jokes in the realm of the spirit when it comes to the use of words.

You cannot utter a negative word in the name of a joke and not expect it to take effect. It will. This is because **words are seeds and the spirit realm is a like fertile ground.** Therefore, *every seed (word) you plant (speak) will reproduce according to its kind.* That is how the effect of words works.

Most times, people unknowingly place themselves, a relationship or marriages under a cloud of curses and in certain situations through the negative effects of their words. When I say unknowingly, I do not mean they do not always understand what they are saying. In most cases, they do.

After all, they put the words together into a sentence and uttered them. But what I mean is that they are unaware of the influence or impact those comments are likely have on them later in the journey of love. That is how many unknowingly deprive themselves of the joy and happiness they desire and deserve.

Though you have the right to speak freely, nothing you say is actually free. Your words always come with unforeseen 'costs'. In my few years of being a Christian, one thing I have come to understand is that ***whatever you curse cannot survive.*** Yes, that is how powerful words are. What you curse may not die instantly, but it will with time.

Remember that when you plant a seed, it does not germinate instantly. It can take days, weeks or even months depending on the type of seed you planted. Words follow the same pattern. To prove the power or effect of words, let us take a look at some few scriptures in the Bible:

*1 In the beginning God created the heaven and the earth. 2 And the earth was without form, and void; and darkness was upon the face of the deep. And the Spirit of God moved upon the face of the waters. 3 **And God said, Let there be light: and there was light.***

Genesis 1:1-3

In this scripture, we see how God brought light into the darkness and void that was on earth when He created it. How did He do it? Words! The Bible says, *"And God said…"* It means God spoke;

He used words, and the effect of those words manifested – it brought light into the darkness.

It means that **words have creative ability.** They can create things that were initially not there. They can produce what is absent. God's words brought into existence creations that were previously not there.

That is exactly what happens when you use words carelessly – they bring into existence bad things. What does the Bible say about Jesus Christ in the New Testament?

> *11 And Jesus entered into Jerusalem, and into the temple: and when he had looked round about upon all things, and now the eventide was come, he went out unto Bethany with the twelve. 12 And on the morrow, when they were come from Bethany, he was hungry:*

> *13 And seeing a fig tree afar off having leaves, he came, if haply he might find any thing thereon: and when he came to it, he found nothing but leaves; for the time of figs was not yet. 14 **And Jesus answered and said unto it, No man eat fruit of thee hereafter for ever. And his disciples heard it.***

> *20 And in the morning, as they passed by, they saw the fig tree dried up from the roots. 21 **And Peter calling to remembrance saith unto him, Master, behold, the fig tree which thou cursedst is withered away.***

Matthew 11:11-14, 20-21

DON'T CURSE YOUR RELATIONSHIP OR MARRIAGE

This is one of the scriptures that readily comes to mind when it comes to the effect or power of the words we utter. One question jumps to mind – *what made the fig tree to dry up from the roots?*

Was it the atmospheric condition? No! Was it that the soil has lost the necessary nutrients to aid the growth of the tree? A big no! So what happened?

It was the effect of the words Jesus spoke to it. The power behind words manifested. This proves that **every word that is spoken has an effect.** Peter said, *"Master, behold, the fig tree which you cursed is withered away."* In other words, the fig tree was growing well until Jesus spoke *against* it. So, Peter was saying, *"Master, the effect of Your words on the fig tree has manifested."*

The fig tree withered because Jesus cursed it means the words Jesus spoke affected the fig tree. The tree reacted to the effect of the words. Jesus' curse took the life out of the tree even though it was still rooted and connected to everything it previously depended on for growth.

That is how powerful words are. They can give life, and they can take life. From these scenario, we can safely deduce that **things take the form of the words we speak to them.** For instance, if you want a dying man to live, you have to be speaking the words of life to him.

With time, he will take on the form of those words as he believes and assimilates them, and live. The effect of those words will manifest in his life. Even though the attention of this book is on relationships and marriages, I must say that its content can be applied to every area of life.

The 'fig tree' could also represent your business, children, education, finances, ministry, etc. If the effect of the words of Christ caused the tree to wither, it tells you what your words can do to these in your life. It is important to also note that *the withering of the tree happened in less than twenty-four hours.*

That means the process began the very moment Jesus uttered the words. I am of the opinion that ***if people learn to bridle their tongues, they will enjoy the glory God has destined for their relationships and marriages***. Yes, there will be challenges, but there will also be God's glory. ***If we will learn to use words positively, we will see their positive effects.***

The truth is that ***you can walk in every level of greatness you desire for your relationship or marriage, but the key is in learning to use your words rightly.*** And it is possible. ***You cannot speak words with negative effects and expect positive results.*** Who plants a mango seed and harvests pawpaw at the end of the day?

Or who plants an orange seed and harvests cassava? According to the word of God, ***every word uttered*** – negative or positive – ***is bound to come to pass with time.***

I believe this is the first truth people must be exposed to after surrendering their lives to Jesus Christ. They must be taught the effect of their words in their new life as Christians to guide them. ***You cannot be speaking anyhow as a Christian and expect to live a victorious and glorious life***. Whatever you say will produce after its kind.

DON'T CURSE YOUR RELATIONSHIP OR MARRIAGE

There is no word the tongue speaks that does not have life. ***Anything you say will surely manifest with time.*** Anything means anything so be careful when you are speaking.

Thou shalt also decree a thing, and it shall be established unto thee: *and the light shall shine upon thy ways.*

Job 22:28

Until you understand this truth, you may never see the need to control the things you say. The fact that something comes to mind does not mean it should be said, especially if it will leave a negative effect. ***Life is primarily destined to give you two things – what you say and what you do.*** You cannot succeed only through your efforts; your words must complement what you do with your effort.

Your words can limit your actions or efforts if they do not carry a positive effect. ***Until your words correlate with what you do, there is no way you will get the result you deserve.*** Before you open your mouth to say anything concerning your relationship or marriage, think about the effect it will have on it.

In the book of Numbers chapters 13 and 14, we read that God instructed Moses to send twelve men, each a leader in the various tribes of Israel, to go and search the land of Canaan and come back with a report. This was the land He promised to give them – a land flowing with milk and honey.

So, Moses in obedience to the commandment of the Lord, sent them into the wilderness. They went up, searched the land, and returned after forty days with their reports. Ten out of the fourteen men came with an evil report, but Joshua and Caleb encouraged the Israelites.

God was greatly displeased with the people because they did not believe in Him despite all the signs and wonders He had performed in their midst. He decided to disown them there and then as a result of their words. But Moses interceded for them and obtained pardon.

Even though the Lord pardoned them on account of Moses, they still paid for the things they said. ***Words are not cheap.*** They can cost you your destiny and everything God has in mind for you.

26 And the LORD spake unto Moses and unto Aaron, saying, 27 How long shall I bear with this evil congregation, which murmur against me? I have heard the murmurings of the children of Israel, which they murmur against me.

28 Say unto them, As truly as I live, saith the LORD, as ye have spoken in mine ears, so will I do to you: *29 Your carcases shall fall in this wilderness; and all that were numbered of you, according to your whole number, from twenty years old and upward, which have murmured against me,*

30 Doubtless ye shall not come into the land, concerning which I sware to make you dwell therein, save Caleb the son of Jephunneh, and Joshua the son of Nun.

31 But your little ones, which ye said should be a prey, them will I bring in, and they shall know the land which ye have despised.

32 But as for you, your carcases, they shall fall in this wilderness. 33

And your children shall wander in the wilderness forty years, and bear your whoredoms, until your carcases be wasted in the wilderness.

34After the number of the days in which ye searched the land, even forty days, each day for a year, shall ye bear your iniquities, even forty years, and ye shall know my breach of promise.

35 I the LORD have said, I will surely do it unto all this evil congregation, that are gathered together against me: in this wilderness they shall be consumed, and there they shall die.

Numbers 14:26-35

Did you see that? The words of these men affected the people of Israel. A journey that should have taken forty days took forty years. Why? Because of what they said; because of the effect of their words.

Can you imagine what your words can do to your destiny, ministry, finances, education, etc.? Do you know that *the delay in the lives of some people are as a result of their words*? Are you aware that some do not have the fruit of the womb because of their words? Be wise!

CHAPTER SIX
WHY RELATIONSHIPS AND MARRIAGES ARE CURSED

C urses, unlike fruits, do not grow on trees. They are often unleashed through words and actions. That means they do not come to the scene until they are invited or unleashed through the words or actions of men.

There are things that trigger people to curse their relationship or marriage. Please, note that the focus of this book is not on what *others* do in an attempt to destroy your relationship or marriage, but on what you do and the reason you do it, knowingly or unknowingly. Let us take a look at a few:

Unmet expectations

It is well-known that people have expectations in a relationship or in marriage. Everybody has a reason behind their decision to fall in love or be with whoever they choose. *What drives people into the 'arms' of others differs from person to person.*

This is a truth some people do not understand and that is how problems usually start in relationships and marriages.

When two people decide to be in a relationship or marry, they each have what they hope to get at the end of the day. *No sane person gets involved with the other in matters of love without a reason.* And this reason(s) differ(s) from one person to the other. From the very moment people decide to fall in love – be in a relationship or marry – there is a 'catch' or reason to it.

This 'catch' or reason behind their desire or decision is what we call an *expectation*. ***An expectation is the feeling that something will or should happen*** –usually something good. But one of the funny things about life is that ***sometimes, things do not turn out exactly the way a person wants or expects***.

As an example, **A** and **B** decide to date or marry. **A** is doing it for deep seated emotional needs and security, and **B** for love and companionship. By implication, what it means is that none of these two would want their expectations for falling in love to fall on the rocks.

As a matter of fact, we can say without doubt that while **A** expects his expectation to be met by **B**, the reverse is also true. Now, what happens when their expectation are not met to their satisfaction? Most times, people resort to the use of wrong words.

When people feel or think their expectations are not being met – whatever they may be – they often speak anyhow about their relationship or marriage. That is one of the reasons people curse their relationships or marriages.

The moment a person feels he is not getting what he wants, he begins to care less about what happens to the relationship or marriage. And once that happens, it is easy to destroy it through wrong words. When you find yourself in such a situation, the best thing to do is to have control over your tongue and actions.

It will go a long way to keep you from cursing your relationship or marriage. ***The virtue required here is patience.*** A relationship or marriage goes through different phases. Remember, ***every relationship or marriage has goes through very unique challenges.***

Therefore, when things are not going the way you expect or planned, be careful not to use any offensive words on your relationship or marriage. It will be a recipe for disaster.

Though you have an expectation for your love life, one thing you need to know and understand is that things will be both *smooth* and *rough* in the journey. There will be periodic bumps along the way.

Sometimes, things will happen at the time you want and at other times too, it will not. That is one of the sad realities about life. Therefore, ***you must understand that the evil words you speak place a limitation on your relationship and marriage.*** The fact that the marriage delayed does not mean you should speak anyhow about the relationship or your partner.

I often tell some of my lady friends that ***there is a difference between a man who has what it takes to marry you but is refusing to, and one who desires to make you his wife but is going through hard times.*** When dealing with the latter, be mindful of your words since they can affect you many years later.

Some people really have what it takes to marry but are reluctant because they just want to use the ladies they are involved with and dump them. That is very wrong. But that is not everybody's mindset. Some people are genuinely going through a tough time so be mindful of your words towards them.

To the men or the husbands, the fact that childbirth has delayed does not mean you should curse your relationship, marriage or your spouse. **Sometimes, the men are the problem, not the women.** So, before you open your mouth to utter anything against your partner, think twice.

It is important to choose your words wisely when dealing with your partner during these trying times.

The things that sometimes happen to people are no fault of theirs. That is life, and we must learn to encourage each other through it.

Whenever you are tempted to speak any word that will curse your relationship or marriage, remember these scriptures:

To every thing there is a season, and a time to every purpose under the heaven:

Ecclesiastes 3:1

11 I returned, and saw under the sun, that the race is not to the swift, nor the battle to the strong, neither yet bread to the wise, nor yet riches to men of understanding, nor yet favor to men of skill; but time and chance happeneth to them all.

*12 **For man also knoweth not his time:** as the fishes that are taken in an evil net, and as the birds that are caught in the snare, even so are the sons of men snared in an evil time, when it falleth suddenly upon them.*

Ecclesiastes 9:11-12 (ASV)

When expectations are not met today, it does not mean they cannot be met tomorrow. You may not have it today, but it does not mean you will never have it. But I can assure you that if you do not learn to bridle your tongue, you can never have it.

In conclusion, ***do you think it is worth cursing your relationship or marriage*** – something you toiled to build over time – ***because you feel your expectations are not being met...yet?*** Why build only to pull it down later with your words or actions? Let wisdom guide your actions and words in life.

Human Difference

Another thing you need to understand is that ***no matter how deep you may be in love, you and your partner are two different people***, even if it is God's *will* for the two of you to be together. ***Whoever you date or marry is a different person.***

For that reason, you will not see things through the same lens always; you will not perceive things at the same level. In other words, ***you will have different perspectives on issues*** and that is fine. It does not however mean that both of you are not compatible.

Two people having the same idea or perspective is not the standard for measuring compatibility when it comes to issues of relationship or marriage. ***You could have the same perspective and still be highly incompatible according to God's plan.***

As a rule of thumb, people in a relationship or who are even married usually have different interests, personalities, expectations, etc., and that is not a bad thing at all. These differences can spice up the love if handled with maturity.

But if things are not managed properly, it could lead to chaos in the home. People do not always marry those they share the same interests with. That rarely happens. That is the reason you need to understand that ***exercising restraint will be a great blessing to your union***. People are different in many ways – *temperament, upbringing, ideology, taste, maturity level, culture, philosophy, fashion taste,* etc.

You can have someone who loves to party involved with someone who does not really like parties and they are cool because they have not allowed their differences to get in their way.

Like I said, human differences can spice up your relationship or marriage when you are both mature. But when the opposite is the case, it will become the bane of it and the doorway to hurts and pain.

It is wrong to use derogatory words on your partner just because he or she does not see something your way. When you do that, it can open the door for curses to be unleashed through words. ***No matter how long you know a person, you cannot know everything about them***.

Being with someone for a long time is not proof or an indication that you have the same interests. There are differences that must be properly managed every step of the way to prevent them from causing problems in the relationship or marriage. When you take a good look at most of the relationships and marriages around today, you will see that people do not know how to manage their differences.

Some people who have been married for decades will tell you that one of the many keys to longevity in marriage is the ability to manage differences. Failing to do this will often lead to hurts and pains that trigger words and actions that debilitate years of efforts. Do not allow the devil to capitalize on your differences to wreck your home. Never give him that chance.

Ignorance and impatience

Another reason many relationships and marriages are cursed is ignorance and impatience. These two are like both sides of a coin and often go hand in hand. Ignorance some say is bliss, but I say if that is true, then that logic does not in any way apply to relationships and marriages.

There is a saying that what you do not know cannot kill you. That is a fool's talk. ***The fact that certain statements sound good to the ears does not mean they make sense.*** They may sound nice, but they are not wise sayings. In fact, those who quote such words do not know how dangerous ignorance is.

To be ignorant is *to lack knowledge or education on a subject*. This doesn't not mean that one does not have knowledge at all; he does but what he knows cannot sustain him. ***What you do not know about marriage or relationship will make you destroy it without even knowing.***

What you do not know will always work to your detriment.

DON'T CURSE YOUR RELATIONSHIP OR MARRIAGE

My people are destroyed for lack of knowledge: because thou hast rejected knowledge, I will also reject thee, that thou shalt be no priest to me: seeing thou hast forgotten the law of thy God, I will also forget thy children.

Hosea 4:6

These are the words of God. He was talking about His children – the Israelites. ***Ignorance was the cause of their destruction***; they rejected knowledge. Do not joke with ignorance. ***What a person does not know can kill him faster than the deadliest potion.*** The right knowledge can save your relationship or marriage.

Many people will tell you they lost good partners as a result of ignorance and impatience. If they had the knowledge they have now, they would not have taken those steps. But it is too late to turn back the hands of time.

There are people who do not know that relationships and marriages must go through processes to become and give them what they expect. As a result, they run it down with their words and actions. ***A woman cannot get pregnant today and deliver tomorrow.*** It is not possible.

Even Jesus Christ had to be carried in the womb for nine months. It means ***pregnancy must go through the necessary stages for delivery***.

And for that to happen, you need a great deal of knowledge and patience. During the stages, there are discomforts – sleepless nights, the development of strange appetites that initially were not there, etc. All these, no matter how discomforting and painful, are necessary to deliver a *sound* baby.

Now, that is how relationships and marriages are designed to work. They must go through processes to become what they have to be. Not knowing this is a recipe for disaster. Do you know that ***a man who lacks patience cannot be a farmer***? This is because it will take some time for the seed he plants to germinate, grow and bear.

If that is the case, then a person who lacks patience and is ignorant is not far from destroying the good things in his relationship or marriage with words. He would not be able to refrain from talking it down because it takes a great deal of patience to do that.

Ignorance has pushed people to speak certain words against their partners. They have erected walls of restriction against their relationships and marriages, and denied themselves progress and happiness in their love lives. *If the people of God are destroyed because of ignorance, imagine what it can do to you.*

Impatience has also made a lot of people to destroy the glorious things God intends to do in their lives. A lot of people have walked out of God ordained relationships and marriages because they could not wait for the time set by God to glorify them.

One of the things partners or couples need is insight into their relationship or marriage. ***It is good to fall in love, but it is not enough.*** After you have fallen in love, do not forget that there are stages you must go through. Both of you must know that it will take work and time to give you what you desire.

DON'T CURSE YOUR RELATIONSHIP OR MARRIAGE

Knowing this can go a long way to save both of you from marring a good thing with your words and actions. *It is very good to learn or read materials on relationship and marriage to cure ignorance, but you have to also be careful about the things you read.* It is not every information out there that is good for consumption.

Without a spoken word, nothing can exist; if you do not speak evil in your relationship or marriage, it will not exist. *Words are the building blocks of all the things we see around us.* Without them, none of the things we see would have existed.

₁In the beginning was the Word, and the Word was with God, and the Word was God. ₂The same was in the beginning with God. ₃All things were made by him; and without him was not any thing made that was made.

John 1:1-3

Words make things. They bring things into existence. Do you know that you create an atmosphere through your words when you speak out of impatience and ignorance? Do you know that you risk the glorious destiny God has in store for you if you are moved by what you do not know to speak anyhow?

But the good news is that there is an antidote for ignorance and that is what this book is presenting to you – insight that comes from the wisdom of God.

Offence and unforgiveness

If you want to be successful in a relationship and/or marriage, *you must know how to handle offence* and *have the heart to forgive*. Anyone who has these qualities is likely to have great control over his tongue and avert a lot of evil.

One thing I want you to understand is that *so long as you are alive and on earth, there is no way you can escape, avoid or prevent offence*. Whether you like it or not, people will offend you in one way or the other.

Then said he unto the disciples, **It is impossible but that offences will come:** *but woe unto him, through whom they come!*

Luke 17:1

Most Christians are victims when it comes to their choice and use of words when they are offended in their relationship or marriage. They speak anyhow without thinking about the impact or effects of their words. Words are not cheap; they are very expensive. This is what the Bible says on the subject:

Just as the Bible says, offences will definitely come. But the question is, *"What should you do when they come?"* The answer is very simple – forgive! Let go! Is it always easy to do that? No! But it is the best thing to do if you intend to keep your relationship or marriage

Forgiveness is the best way to go if your marriage means anything to you. Do you know the number of people who have lost great and wonderful partners to unforgiveness?

DON'T CURSE YOUR RELATIONSHIP OR MARRIAGE

Sometimes, no matter how you exercise caution in dealing with people, you will either hurt them or be hurt by them. Such is life. That is why forgiveness is necessary.

I know it can sometimes be difficult to forgive some things but for the sake of what you have, learn to let things go.

I discovered something profound about Jesus Christ when He was being crucified. The Bible says when they came to Calvary where He was put on the cross with the two other evil-doers, He did something.

Then said Jesus, **Father, forgive them; for they know not what they do.** *And they parted his raiment, and cast lots.*

Luke 23:34

One of the lessons I have learnt from this story is that ***sometimes, those who offend or hurt us do not know what they are doing.*** I know this cannot be said of everybody, but ***there are some people who genuinely do not know that they have stepped on your toe.***

I am not talking about people who know what they have done but are too proud to accept their faults or even apologize. Every now and then, we meet these kind of people in our lives.

I am also not talking about those who will go any length to defend a foolish act because they think it will make them less of a person when they accept their fault and render an apology.

I am talking about those who do not have the slightest idea that something they said or did has offended you. ***One of the things*** *that strikes my mind in the prayer Jesus prayed for these people is that they did not even ask to be forgiven.*

The Bible explicitly tells us that they did not know what they were doing. What lesson does that teach us? *People must not be forgiven only when they ask.* There are people who refuse to forgive their partners an offence because they did not ask for it. But wait! How can a person ask to be forgiven for something they are not even aware they have done?

And even if they are, must you wait to be asked before you let it go? *A person asking for forgiveness is not necessarily a sign that he is truly remorseful.* That is the reason *forgiveness must not be based on a condition.* You can let your partner know how an action or a word they said has hurt or offended you.

She/he may accept their fault and apologize. On the other hand, she or he may challenge your claim. But beloved, do what Jesus did on the cross of Calvary – let it go. *Is what you have to protect not important that keeping scores?*

As humans, we can be tempted to think that taking revenge is the best thing to do. It is not! As a matter of fact, that is how many people lost their marriages and relationships. *The need to seek revenge can blind you to what you stand to lose in the end.* And most times, people come to this realization too late.

Forgiveness can change a bad thing into a good one. The opposite is also true. *Forgiveness can roll away the atmosphere of tension and gloom in your home.* But unforgivness on the other hand will open the floodgates of trouble into your home and wash away peace.

DON'T CURSE YOUR RELATIONSHIP OR MARRIAGE

When unforgiveness lurks in your heart, it slowly poisons it against your relationship or marriage. It becomes the source of the evil or bad experiences you encounter in life. *Holding on to offence is like taking a coal of fire in your hands.* It can transform a beautiful thing into an ugly one. It can quench the light of your destinies and erect stumbling blocks against your joy and happiness.

One of the greatest weapons you can use against the devil is forgiveness – letting go of offences. *When you develop the heart of forgiveness, you displace the seat of the devil in the affairs of your love life.* You kick him out and give him no room to function or operate.

Sometimes in a relationship or marriage, there are moments of disappointment and pain. Those who refuse to forgive or let go of these things end up making room for the devil to walk in and have a feast. And one thing I know is that *wherever the devil feasts, he leaves a mess.*

Nobody wants these unpleasant moments in their love life, but they sometimes creep in on you. The best you can do when they come is to develop a heart that easily forgives. In conclusion, I want you to understand that *people do not utter offensive words because they are hurt; they do because they failed to forgive.*

Anger

This is the major cause of curses in relationships and marriages and most people do not even know it. *Can you remember any time you or a friend spoke while angry? What did you or that friend say? Were the words pleasant to the ears? What came to your mind when you were saying those words?*

If I am not wrong, you probably thought or felt you were pouring out your emotions. But little did you know that you were doing more than that – that you were unleasing curses through the medium of that anger with your words.

People normally lose consciousness when they are angry and that is how they often spew curses. When you are upset, do you control your tongue or you allow it to control you? Are you aware that **unless one gains mastery over his emotions, it is relatively easier to use offensive words when he is angry**?

People tend to forget who they are and only focus on voicing out the way they feel. But what does the Bible teach us about being angry?

> 26 **Be ye angry, and sin not**: *let not the sun go down upon your wrath:* 27 *Neither give place to the devil.*

Ephesians 4:26-27

One lesson we can learn from the scripture we just read is that **anger may be inevitable**. In this verse, the Bible does not restrict us from getting angry. Why? We are human beings and have emotions.

Rather, the Bible says **if you even get angry, there is a line you are not permitted to cross** – the line into sin. It means there must be a boundary to your anger. There are times certain situations press you so hard that you end up losing your cool. But even so, you are not permitted to utter anything suffocative in your relationship or marriage.

We all get angry sometimes, but the word of God admonishes us to control ourselves when we do so that it does not lead us into sin. Though it sounds impossible, it is very possible to be angry and not sin. How? By restraining yourself and learning to forgive.

What sin is the Bible talking about in the text we just read in Ephesians? It is the sin of abusing words to destroy what God has done and what He is doing in your relationship, marriage, business, finances, etc.

It is doing *anything* that goes against the word of God. ***Being angry is not an excuse to use unwholesome words or lose control of your tongue.*** You give the devil place in your relationship or marriage to mar the happiness and joy God has destined for your union when you speak unwholesome words.

That is the reason it is your duty to make sure you do not give him a place to cause havoc, hurt, and pain. ***You give him foothold when you permit him through your words.*** Watch your words! A fool is known by his anger and words.

> ***He that is soon angry dealeth foolishly:*** *and a man of wicked devices is hated.*

> **Proverbs 14:17**

Anger can make noble people act in a foolish way. It makes them to lose all sense of judgement. ***In a state of anger, people often act foolishly*** and one of the manifestations is firing wrong words.

*19 Wherefore, my beloved brethren, **let every man be swift to hear, slow to speak, slow to wrath:** 20 For the wrath of man worketh not the righteousness of God.*

James 1:19-20

The anger of man only destroys what God has done. The tongue must be a tool for praising what God has done, establishing it, and destroying the works of Satan. Never are you supposed to use the tongue against your destiny.

I have often said that ***it is better to marry a prostitute who has control over her anger than a virgin who cannot control her tongue,*** and I say this advisedly. You are probably wondering the reason I said that, right? Let us take a look at another scripture in the Bible:

Like a city whose walls are broken through is a person who lacks self control.

Proverbs 25:28

Did you see that? What do you think will happen to a city whose walls are broken through? For one, it will lose its protection and enemies will plunder all its wealth and maim and kill its people. Such a city cannot defend itself from any attack.

Is that the kind of marriage you want? Is that the type of relationship you desire? Oftentimes, ***people do not think about the long term effect of the things they say or do when they are angry.*** How many promising relationships and marriages have ended due to words spoken in anger? How many people have driven God-given partners away because of anger?

I guess you can see the great havoc anger can cause when it is not checked. Be vigilant and guard your heart to not curse your life and destiny when you are angry. *When you are in the habit of standing against what God has done for and in your life through your words, you can never know and experience true joy in relationship or marriage.*

Things may not be as blissful as you would have wanted, but never speak against it. Man or woman, husband or wife, you must work on your heartbeat because it is one of Satan's greatest weapons against relationships and marriages in this end time. So, do not think you are use saying words; be careful.

Always remember that ***anger will make you speak foolish words that would destroy your relationship or marriage in the long run.*** Please read that again and make sure it sinks in. Through anger, a lot of people have destroyed the good things God has in store for them even in their lives.

Some people suffering in marriage today destroyed what God was doing in their relationship through anger, and they do not even know it. But they are blaming Him for not giving them the best. How can God not give you the best? Get this - one of the powerful weapons the devil is using in these last days is anger. With this weapon, he has destroyed the destinies of great marriages and relationships.

He has succeeded in bringing beautiful relationships and marriages to nothing by encouraging people to speak evil words in anger.

Not all marriages are destroyed through adultery, fornication, or any other unpleasant thing you can imagine. Some are simply pulled down through the unskilled use of words through anger. It is for this reason that the word of God explicitly warns us against the use of idle words (**Matthew 12:36**).

An idle word is a word that does not encourage. *No matter how angry you may be, you must be very cautious about how you use words.* Do not curse your partner because of anger. *Some marriages may never rise to their destined heights because they were cursed during the period of relationship*. The destinies of those marriages were stagnated through the unskilled use of words in anger.

If you do not know how to control your tongue when you are angry, you cannot enjoy the goodness of God in your union. That is why I often say that *a man's greatest enemy is his words, not the devil.* As a matter of fact *anybody who abuses words is his own enemy.* He will ultimately abuse his destiny. There are no two ways about that. Speaking evil about your relationship or marriage is like stabbing your heart with a knife. How can you survive?

To keep the devil out of your relationship marriage, education, and all that concerns you, learn to speak right. *Kill your anger before it kills what you love* – your relationship or marriage.

DON'T CURSE YOUR RELATIONSHIP OR MARRIAGE

Anger should not under any circumstance cause you to speak evil about anything that concerns your life.

I am perfectly aware that *it may sometimes not be easy to keep quiet when you are angry, but you have to try your best because of your destiny and future*. It is the best way to save what God has destined for your union.

Satan may not get you through the sins we are often cautious of – fornication, stealing, adultery, etc., but he could get you through your anger. Beware!

Anybody who does not know how to control his tongue when angry cannot see good things in life no matter the effort he puts in. Would you like to be in a relationship with or be married to someone like that? Do you think someone would like to be with you if you are like that? Do you know that we are even warned in the Bible to not let the sun go down on our anger?

"In your anger do not sin": **Do not let the sun go down while you are still angry**

Ephesians 4:26 (NIV)

This is what the Bible says. But are you aware that some people sometimes hold on to anger for days, weeks, months and even years? That is not healthy for any relationship or marriage. Keep the devil out of business in your life by subduing anger.

It is one of the keys to enjoying the great fruits and provisions of God for your love life. *Your tongue directs the course or direction of your life*. Check it! Do not give the devil a foothold in your life.

Do not permit him through anger to interfere in the glorious thing God is doing in your life. Anytime you get angry, remember that it is the catalyst for setbacks, failure, etc. Get rid of it!

Unchecked heart and lips

An unchecked heart is a lose canon and can wreck great havoc. This is what the Bible says about the heart:

Keep thy heart with all diligence; for out of it are the issues of life.

Proverbs 4:23

The heart of man controls the affairs of his life. Out of it proceed things like anger, envy, hurt, jealousy, etc. ***A good heart makes for a better life and an evil heart destroys every good thing in a person's life.*** A person gets angry in the heart, not his mind. ***It is the heart that affects the course of a man's life.***

What it means is that *anything that comes into your heart has the power to change the entire direction of your life for good or evil.* That is the reason the Bible is telling you to *keep* your heart with all diligence. That means the onus is on you.

To keep means to protect or to guard. Therefore, ***to keep your heart means to consciously protect or guard it to ensure that the fruits thereof do not destroy the good things God has in store for you.*** Why must you protect your heart?

You must because ***the heart can either build you into your destiny and greatness or take you out or away from it.*** In other words, ***anybody who fails to protect his heart is failing to protect*** *his life.* Protecting the heart is very important because *words are formed in the heart but spoken through the mouth.* Let us take a look at what the Bible says:

O generation of vipers, how can ye, being evil, speak good things? for out of the abundance of the heart the mouth speaketh.

Matthew 12:34

What this scripture means is that *the heart is the foundation of a man's life.* It is a bank of words. A merry heart speaks good words and an evil heart utters evil words. *A good heart can be corrupted when it is not protected.* How true this statement is!

Therefore, it is important to protect it from speaking evil about your life, business, relationship, and/or marriage no matter the circumstance.

43 For a good tree bringeth not forth corrupt fruit; neither doth a corrupt tree bring forth good fruit. 44 For every tree is known by his own fruit. For of thorns men do not gather figs, nor of a bramble bush gather they grapes.

45 A good man out of the good treasure of his heart bringeth forth that which is good; and an evil man out of the evil treasure of his heart bringeth forth that which is evil: for of the abundance of the heart his mouth speaketh.

Luke 6:43-45

The state of a man's heart is the greatest determinant of his life. *Until you master the art of using words skillfully, you cannot become the master of your destiny.* If you want to be great, know how to use words properly. Protect and manage your heart.

Just as a bullet does not consider what it is aimed at to decide whether to come out of the chamber of a gun or not, words do not consider the mood in which they were spoken or uttered. They will either build or destroy whatever they are directed at.

And since the mouth speaks what is in the heart, you will experience what the mouth speaks in your life. What is your heart producing for your mouth to say or utter? Is it good or bad? *Most people do not know that their love life cannot work as a result of what they say about it from their heart.* You have to understand that you are establishing whatever you say with your mouth.

Please, understand that *whatever you declare must be established*. That is the rule of words. And you cannot have the opposite of what you say either.

Death and life are in the power of the tongue, and those who love it will eat its fruit.

Proverbs 18:21 (NASB)

The tongue is powerless without the heart. *It is the heart that fuels, empowers or feeds the tongue what to say at any given time.* So, the 'power in the tongue' refers to the words in the heart of man that are spoken by the tongue (**Matthew 12:34**). That is the reason the tongue is powerless without the heart.

DON'T CURSE YOUR RELATIONSHIP OR MARRIAGE

The words of the tongue either bring life or death. That means they produce their results after their kind. *You don't speak or utter death and expect to live.*

When you declare death, you die or cease to live. *Whatever you say becomes what you get.* So, you have to be careful about what you are planting with your words.

With the fruit of a man's mouth his stomach will be satisfied; He will be satisfied with the product of his lips

Proverbs 18:20 (NASB)

When you understand this truth, you are set to live a victorious life. What are your lips producing into your relationship or marriage? With what are you being satisfied? What words does your mouth speak during the challenging times in your relationship or marriage?

Do you rain curses on your partner and later expect him or her to be a better person for you? Do you curse your relationship or marriage and still expect it to be a source of joy and happiness? It does not work that way.

Your relationship or marriage is bound by your words to be what you say. If your relationship is not working as you expect, check how you speak about it. If your marriage is not giving you the fruits you desire, check the seeds you are planting.

This may seem very insignificant but it is destroying the joy, happiness and blessings of many homes. A cursed relationship will ultimately lead to a cursed marriage. *You cannot plant thorns and expect to harvest grapes*. No matter how I think about it, I can never find a scenario where that is possible.

Some people cannot understand the reason there is no understanding between them and their partners when they believe and constantly say they can never understand each other. *You cannot understand a partner when you think or believe you cannot.*

Cast out misunderstanding with the power of your words. Uproot it from the root and burn its branches with positive confessions. *God did not give us the tongue to curse our lives and what He has done*, but rather to praise and magnify His perfect works in our lives.

If what you declare with your tongues is what will come to pass, then why don't you rather promote your life with your words? *It is not right to speak evil about your partner under any circumstance.* Your words can destroy what God is doing in your life.

It may surprise you to know that *God respects the words from our hearts and implements them.*

At any given moment in a person's life, there are two forces at work to enforce the decrees that proceed out of his mouth – *the angels of God* and *the demons of Satan*. The angels enforce positive declarations whereas demons enforce negative words.

Do you know that *you activate either the ministry of angels or demons by the way you speak?* Your life is never different from your words. God respects whatever you say with your tongue;

that is the reason it will be established. *You are rejecting God when you speak contrary to what He has done for you.* His plan and perfect work concerning your life.

When you speak good things even in the challenging times of your relationship or marriage, you pave way for God to step in and turn the situation around to your favour. But when you utter negative words (curses), you restrain Him from coming in to make things better.

Shortsightedness

Sight refers to how far a person can see and it plays a very important role in relationships and marriages. *How far you can see determines how well you will comport yourself through the storms of your love life.*

One of the greatest challenges about relationships and marriages is that *most people are grown, but only a few are mature.* Growth and maturity are not the same, and the latter is a reflection of how far one can see.

We read earlier that at the command of God, Moses sent twelve men, each from the tribes of Israel to go and spy out the land of Canaan – the land He was giving to them as an inheritance (**Numbers 13:1-3, 17-33**). Each of these men was a leader in their tribe. After the forty days of spying out the land, they came to present their reports (**Numbers 13:25-26**).

This is where something very interesting happened. Out of the twelve, ten came with bad reports. But Joshua and Caleb presented good reports about the land. In the heat of everything,

God spoke and what He said was very frightening. These were His words to the ten men who went to spy out the land with Joseph and Caleb:

"Say to them, 'As I live, says the LORD, ***just as you have spoken in my hearing, so I will surely do to you.***

Numbers 14:28 (NASB)

Did you see God's response to their reports? What this simply means is that when you curse your life, relationship or marriage, business, ministry, etc., there is nothing God can do than to bring to pass what you have said. ***When dealing with God, your words are your possessions***. What you say is what you will get. Never forget that!

In other words, ***you establish your doom or freedom by the words that proceed out of your mouth***. The truth is that the report of the ten leaders was in fact a reflection of the true picture on the ground. But they were not to talk that way. You may be asking yourself why that is so.

First of all, they were leaders and are not supposed to be shortsighted. Secondly, they were of God; they carried His nature and ability inside them. They were descendants of Adam and anything they said had to be established. ***The ten leaders were shortsighted and God was not happy with that.*** Sometimes, in a God-given relationship or marriage, you may see certain signs that prove things may not work.

But be very careful of what you say. ***God may not overlook the pain and hurt from which you spoke***. He will do just as you have spoken into His ears. *When the ten spies reported exactly what they saw on the ground, little did they know that they were expressing doubt in the ability of God.*

The story of your relationship or marriage may be like that of the Israelites. God promised them a land blessed with milk and honey, but *He never told them about the battles they had to fight in order to possess the land.*

But since God was giving the Israelites a land that was been inhabited by their enemies, it means they had what it took to defeat them and to possess it. It means the promise of the inheritance was within reach. What lesson can we learn from the experience of these young men?

God can give you a partner, but He may never tell you what you will go through together in order to enjoy what He has destined for you. And because many do not know that what they see as a problem is part of God's will to give them His best, they talk foolishly. That is the definition of shortsightedness. God is watching and listening.

You may not be happy now with the person God has brought into your life, but be careful you do not speak foolishly. In fact, just shut up if you have nothing better to say! You may think that she or he does not possess the qualities or bodily features you want.

You might think that the person is not good for you and lose hope, but be careful you do not utter any foolish words. *When God is involved, it cannot be a mistake that you are with that person* so just keep mute. Let us take a look at what these men brought upon themselves and their families through their words:

29 *Your corpses shall fall in the wilderness, even all your numbered men, according to your complete number from twenty years old upward,* **who have grumbled against Me.** 30 *Surely,* **you shall not come into the land in which I swore to settle you,** *except Caleb the son of Jephunneh and Joshua the son of Nun*

35 *I the Lord have spoken, surely this I will do to all this evil congregation who are gathered against Me. In the wilderness they shall be destroyed, and there they shall die.*

Numbers 14:29-30, 35

The entire nation suffered for their action and words. It is obvious that they opted to die in the wilderness and also ended their posterity through their words. **They denied themselves, their children and tribes the opportunity to make it into the promised land.** They cut short their destination and that of other generations.

In fact, they cursed their promised land. **Their words changed the course of their lives in God.** That is the power behind the words we speak. Challenges in relationships or marriages are temporal. They are mountains that will not be there forever if only you will learn to make good use of your words.

And Jesus said unto them, Because of your unbelief: for verily I say unto you, If ye have faith as a grain of mustard seed, ye shall say unto this mountain, Remove hence to yonder place; and it shall remove; and nothing shall be impossible unto you.

DON'T CURSE YOUR RELATIONSHIP OR MARRIAGE

Matthew 17:20

Even though challenges may appear as mountains, they will be reduced to molehills with time when partners grow and mature together. *The higher you go in maturity, the smaller they become.* Maturity is important in the journey of love. *Do not be like the ten spies who spoke idle words* and were called out by God to give account for those words.

Keep yourself from speaking carelessly. *If you can control your tongue, you will go far in life.* If you can control your heart and actions, you can control the destiny of your relationship and/or marriage. *Words can be an asset or a liability to you.*

36 And I say to you, that every careless word that men shall speak, they shall render account for it on the day of judgement. 37 For by your words you shall be justified, and by your words you shall be condemned.

Matthew 12:36-37

Wrong words in times of pain and hurt are careless words. They do not and cannot yield any good result. *Every word you speak must be spoken carefully.* In the end, they must yield Godly results. If your words in your trying and challenging moments will not yield a positive result, then do not speak them. Swallow them.

No matter how hurt you think you are, check your heart and lips. Refrain from spitting out careless words. Just shut up! I have observed over time that some people are quick to blame others for being the reason they utter obscenities in their relationship or marriage instead of admitting they were wrong.

The questions are these: *"Who controls your heart? Are others in charge of your tongue and words? Do people think for you or tell you what to say?"* Think about it. Honestly speaking, **you decide on how to respond to the actions of others.** The power is in your hands.

You cannot blame others for how you chose to behave or respond to something they have done. Anytime you are tempted to speak foolishly about your relationship or marriage, remember that God fulfilled the words of the ten spies many years later. Only Joshua and Caleb with their tribes entered the land.

God promised to do what they said into His ears, and He did it. He is a God who keeps His promise. **Do not curse your relationship or marriage;** He will bring it to pass. I marvel at the way people condemn cheating but do nothing about speaking offensive words in their relationships or marriages. Is it because they do not know the dangers or they think they are just expressing emotions?

If only they knew that curses are being released in the process. *It is better to be silent when you are angry if you know you cannot speak right in order to save or preserve your life.* That is a wise thing to do. It does not however mean you cannot let people know when they hurt you or step on your toe.

Speak out and let people know when they hurt you, but in a genuine and sincere spirit without uttering words that will affect your joy and happiness later in life. It takes a lot of maturity to be able to do this and to not stain your destiny with your words.

Do not ensnare yourself with your words from an unchecked heart. It is dangerous. Be determined to have mastery over your heart and tongue to enjoy your union despite all odds. ***Until you gain mastery of your tongue, you cannot gain mastery of your life.*** The direction of your life is determined by your tongue. Look at the power of the tongue:

*5 Even so **the tongue is a little member, and boasteth great things.** Behold, **how great a matter a little fire kindleth!** 6 And the tongue is a fire, a world of iniquity: so is the tongue among our members, that it defileth the whole body, and setteth on fire the course of nature; and it is set on fire of hell.*

*7 For every kind of beasts, and of birds, and of serpents, and of things in the sea, is tamed, and hath been tamed of mankind: 8 But **the tongue can no man tame; it is an unruly evil, full of deadly poison.** 9 Therewith bless we God, even the Father; and therewith curse we men, which are made after the similitude of God.*

10 Out of the same mouth proceedeth blessing and cursing. My brethren, these things ought not so to be. 11 Doth a fountain send forth at the same place sweet water and bitter? 12 Can the fig tree, my brethren, bear olive berries? either a vine, figs? so can no fountain both yield salt water and fresh.

James 3:5-12

Do you see what James has to say about the tongue? No amount of words can explain the impact, effect and importance of words on your relationship and/or marriage as a child of God. Even so, do not let negative words show you such effects. Throughout the Bible, **the word of God explains and shows us that there is power in our words.** Let us take a look at a few of them:

The discretion of a man deferreth his anger; and it is his glory to pass over a transgression.

Proverbs 19:11

20 **He that handleth a matter wisely shall find good:** *and whoso trusteth in the LORD, happy is he. 21 The wise in heart shall be called prudent: and the sweetness of the lips increaseth learning.*

22 Understanding is a wellspring of life unto him that hath it: but the instruction of fools is folly. 23 **The heart of the wise teacheth his mouth, and addeth learning to his lips. 24 Pleasant words [are as] an honeycomb, sweet to the soul, and health to the bones.**

25 There is a way that seemeth right unto a man, but the end thereof are the ways of death. 26 He that laboureth laboureth for himself; for his mouth craveth it of him. 27 An ungodly man diggeth up evil: **and in his lips there is as a burning fire.**

Proverbs 16:20-27

20 A man's belly shall be satisfied with the fruit of his mouth; and with the increase of his lips shall he be filled. 21 Death and life are

DON'T CURSE YOUR RELATIONSHIP OR MARRIAGE

in the power of the tongue: and they that love it shall eat the fruit thereof.

Proverbs 18:20-21

Long before Jesus came into the scene, the author of the book of Proverbs wrote the words above. In fact, other authors in the Bible also spoke on the subject. Jesus Christ confirmed what was written in the New Testament one day when He spoke these words:

*33 Either make the tree good, and his fruit good; or else make the tree corrupt, and his fruit corrupt: for the tree is known by his fruit. 34 **O generation of vipers, how can ye, being evil, speak good things? for out of the abundance of the heart the mouth speaketh.***

35 A good man out of the good treasure of the heart bringeth forth good things: and an evil man out of the evil treasure bringeth forth evil things.

*36 But I say unto you, That **every idle word that men shall speak, they shall give account thereof in the day of judgment.** 37 For by thy words thou shalt be justified, and by thy words thou shalt be condemned*

Matthew 12:33-37

The tree represents your relationship or marriage. The fruits represent what they have to offer – the benefits. So, the good fruits mean good things and the bad fruits represents bad things.

Now, ***it is the things you say*** (the words from your mouth) ***that fertilizes and determines the kind of fruits the tree*** (relationship or marriage) ***produces.***

In other words, you determine what you experience – good or bad. This is one of the truths you need to understand about your relationship or marriage if you are going to see and enjoy good fruits. That is the reason Apostle Paul has this to say:

*29 **Let no evil word come out of your mouths,** but only such as is good for edifying, as fits the occasion, that it may impart grace to those who hear. 30 And do not grieve the Holy Spirit of God, in whom you were sealed for the day of redemption*

*31 **Let all bitterness and wrath and anger and clamor and slander be put away from you, with all malice,** 32 And be kind to one another, tenderhearted, **forgiving one another,** as God in Christ forgave you.*

Ephesians 4:29-32 (RSV)

It seems as though it is natural for men to speak evil when they are hurt or in pain. But it is not; it is a demonic act. ***The Spirit of God does not speak evil.*** Apostle Paul led by the Holy Spirit in his writing to the church at Ephesus admonished and commanded them to not speak evil words because he knew the consequences.

The devil has work to do in your relationship and/or marriage only when you employ him by your evil words. So, in order to keep him unemployed and to render him useless in the affairs of your life, only speak good words that will edify you to work on and overcome the challenges you encounter.

Apostle Paul also spoke about not grieving the Holy Spirit. How do we grieve Him? One of the ways is by speaking evil or negative words about ourselves. It means even God is not happy when we express negative thoughts about His plan for our lives.

What is the remedy to this problem or challenge? Simple - constantly speak positive words no matter the challenges you encounter on the journey.

Negative words about your relationship or marriage surely grieves Him. This also applies to anything that concerns your life or destiny. ***Learn to speak positively in the face of adversity.*** Put aside anger or wrath.

Putting aside anger is the same as doing away with evil words or curses. ***When you hold on to anger, it provokes evil thoughts in your heart which inspires evil words.*** And those evil words once spoken mars the destiny of your relationship or marriage.

If you love what God has given you and value it so much, then always choose your words carefully when speaking about it. Don't look down on the power of your words. Instead of using it negatively, use it for your good.

CHAPTER SEVEN

REDEEMING A CURSED RELATIONSHIP OR MARRIAGE

If you have come this far with reading this book, I believe you have realized that somewhere along the line, you *may* have cursed your relationship and/or marital destiny unknowingly.

Though it is easier and faster to pull down what you have built over the years through your words, the good news is that it can be rebuilt with dedication and diligence. Yes, there is hope.

This book has spoken extensively on the power of words and it is only good to tell you how you can redeem that which is cursed. It might require a lot of work and consciousness depending on how long it has been knee-deep in curses, but you can do it. All you have to do is the following:

• Use the power of prayer and positive words to right every negative word you, your partner or others have ever spoken against your love life.

• Learn to have control over your heart, especially when angry - **Proverbs 25:28**

• Speak positive words over your relationship or marriage always – **Job 28:23**

DON'T CURSE YOUR RELATIONSHIP OR MARRIAGE

• Seek God's wisdom in dealing with your partner or spouse and the challenges that confront you on the journey of love – **James 1:2-5**

• Lean to appreciate your partner and make an effort to protect what you have consciously.

• Seek the Lord for insight and revelation as to how you can come out of the curses that are entangling your relationship or marriage – **Jeremiah 33:3**

• Ask God to prompt or show you the instances you used words to curse your relationship, marriage, education, finances, children, etc. and consciously reverse them.

ARE YOU BORN AGAIN

God bless you for making time to read this book. I hope you enjoyed it and the contents have refreshed, rejuvenated, blessed and impacted your life positively.

Though this book has been a great blessing, it cannot compare to the immense blessing God has in store for you through the person of Jesus Christ. Look at what the Bible says about God's love for you:

For God so loved the world, that he gave his only begotten Son, that whosoever believeth in him should not perish, but have everlasting life.

John 3:16

This scripture simply means that God loves you so much that He sent Jesus Christ into the world to die for you. The truth is that He has always loved you and is patiently waiting for you to accept His love into your heart. How do you accept this sweet love of God into your heart?

All you have to do is ask His Son, Jesus Christ, to come into your heart and to be the Lord and Saviour of your life *(if you have never done that)*. But if you have and for some reasons there is the need for you to rededicate your life to Him, please do not hesitate to do so. It is very important.

DON'T CURSE YOUR RELATIONSHIP OR MARRIAGE

Say this prayer from your heart sincerely to Jesus Christ – as a man speaks to his friend – meaning every word:

God, I am a sinner and I cannot save myself. The Bible says in John 3:16 that You love me and that is why You sent Jesus Christ to come and die in my place for my sins on the cross.

Jesus, You died, You were buried in a tomb and on the third day, You resurrected from the dead. By faith, I accept what You did for me through Your death and resurrection.

I confess You as the Lord and Saviour of my life

and receive Your love into my heart. Be the Lord and King over my life from today. Teach me, guide me and help me to live a holy life for You alone all the days of my life.

Thank you for accepting me as Your child.

If you prayed this prayer sincerely, you are specially welcome into the blessed and wonderful family of God. I assure you that you will never regret this decision as you diligently follow God's word and leading and plan for your life.

You are set for greater things in life! God bless you!

ABOUT THE AUTHOR

WISDOM REALMS is an author, the CEO of Wisdom Realms Publications *(a company that publishes Christian materials to nourish the church)*, the visionary of Wisdom Realms Impact Project, songwriter, teacher of the word, worship leader and a messenger of God with the heart and passion for revival.

Called as an evangelist, he is sent with a defined commission – *to help prune and prepare the church for the second coming of our Lord and Saviour Jesus Christ* – one he has been very committed to wholeheartedly over the years through his messages and writings.

With the unique and strong teaching unction and apostolic grace upon his life, he communicates the mysteries of God's kingdom and His unadulterated word in simple language to the understanding of men.

He preaches, teaches and writes with the fire and passion of the Holy Spirit. His messages focus on the church, purpose, faith in God, holiness, commitment to God, righteousness, and discipline in the body of Christ.

His greatest heart desires is to be used of God to spread the word of salvation and to be an instrument of deliverance unto those who are under the bondage of the devil – the very mandate of his call.

As a preacher and a teacher, he longs to see the day when God's revival will hit the Church again in an unusual way and like a torrential flood, sweep across all the nations of the earth before the glorious coming of Jesus Christ, the King of kings and Lord of lords.

OTHER BOOKS BY THE AUTHOR

Don't miss out!

Visit the website below and you can sign up to receive emails whenever Wisdom Realms publishes a new book. There's no charge and no obligation.

https://books2read.com/r/B-A-CKXAB-MNOQC

BOOKS 2 READ

Connecting independent readers to independent writers.

Also by Wisdom Realms

Lessons From Joseph's Life (Growth and Nourishment Through Life's Experiences)
Wisdom for the Day (Your Daily Dose of God's Wisdom...)
Don't Curse Your Relationship or Marriage